SOUL INVASION STUDY GUIDE

D1213683

TABLE
OF
CONTENTS

FRONT MATTER

SMALL GROUP/LEADER HELPS

WELCOME

TROY BREWER

Welcome to *Soul Invasion*. I'd like you to stop for a moment and think about those two words "soul" and "invasion." Can you define each of them? I can promise you this: by the end of this study you will not think of either of those words the same way you do today. God's Word is going to change your thinking.

Actually, God's Word is going to invade your thinking. Right now, you may have a captive mind and not even realize it. Even as a believer you may be stuck in the old dominion that ruled your life before Jesus. Look at what Jesus spelled out as the remedy for that bondage.

Then Jesus said to those Jews who believed Him, "If you abide in My word, you are My disciples indeed. And you shall know the truth, and

the truth shall make you free." (John 8:31-32 NKJV).

What did Jesus say would make us free? The difference between being in bondage and being set free is knowing the truth. It's not the truth that makes us free; it is knowing the truth that makes us free. Being set free and walking in victory is a matter of what you know.

I believe with all my heart that a lot of Christians are seeing the best part of their life corrupted, dishonored, degraded, and ruined simply because they don't know how to confront the beast. Instead of being led by the Spirit of God, we tend to be driven by terrible thinking patterns that need to be invaded and taken over by the Word of Almighty God.

SOUL INVASION is meant to be an arsenal for you to defeat the enemy. If you want to have victory in a way the world does not, you have to think different than the world does! The Bible gives real strategies on how to think in difficult times when the voice of the enemy (or the in-a-me) comes upon you.

If you have victory controlling your thoughts, you will inevitably have victory over your feelings, because your thoughts control your feelings. Feelings tend to influence your actions. Having real victory in your thoughts is the key to changing your whole life. During this study, God wants to get a hold of your life like He never has. To do this, He needs to get a hold of your mind like He never has. You get your life transformed by getting your mind renewed and that can only happen when God invades it.

And do not be conformed to this world, but be transformed by the renewing of your mind, that you may prove what is that good and acceptable and perfect will of God... (Romans 12:2 NKJV).

Troy Brewer

USING
THIS
GUIDE

Developed as a companion for Troy Brewer's book *Soul Invasion: Biblical Strategies for Victorious Living*, this guide has been designed for use by individuals as well as groups to study the Bible's teaching on the part of our soul that thinks. The way you think affects everything else: "***For as he thinks in his heart, so is he.***" (Proverbs 23:7a NKJV).

Individual Study: Cover one lesson at a time and move at your own pace.

Group Study: Plan to cover at least one lesson each time you meet. Encourage everyone to read the book and prepare for the discussion. Choose a few key questions from the lesson to discuss with the group— there will be plenty to talk about.

Lesson Structure – Each lesson includes the following parts as suggested steps for engaging with the biblical content and Troy's teaching in *Soul Invasion*. The following sequence will be used:

Related reading in *Soul Invasion* – The relevant pages from the book will be noted.

Warm-up: Scripture and Brief Meditation/Question – Each lesson begins with a thought-provoking passage from the Bible and a brief meditation and/or question about the content of the lesson.

Read the Assignment: Get in the habit of either reading the assigned chapter before you do the lesson, or at this point. Underline your book and use the note space provided to jot significant page numbers, Scripture references, or notes to self.

Notice Questions: What you learned and remember – the first set of questions will allow you to review your awareness of the teaching and note truth for future action.

Think Questions: What you understand and realize – the second set of questions will explore the significance of the teaching and the applicable principles from God's Word.

Apply Questions: How you will apply the truth you know – the third set of questions will guide you toward making some specific decisions about applying the truth of the lesson to your life.

Move Toward Freedom – A final thought/challenge from Pastor Troy.

The Lord is my shepherd;
I shall not want.
He makes me to lie down in green pastures;
He leads me beside the still waters.
He restores my soul;
He leads me in the paths of righteousness
For His name's sake.
Yea, though I walk through the valley of the shadow of dea
I will fear no evil;
For You are with me;
Your rod and Your staff, they comfort me.
You prepare a table before me in the presence of my ener
You anoint my head with oil;
My cup runs over.
Surely goodness and mercy shall follow me
All the days of my life;
And I will dwell in the house of the Lord Forever.

PSALMS 23 NKJV

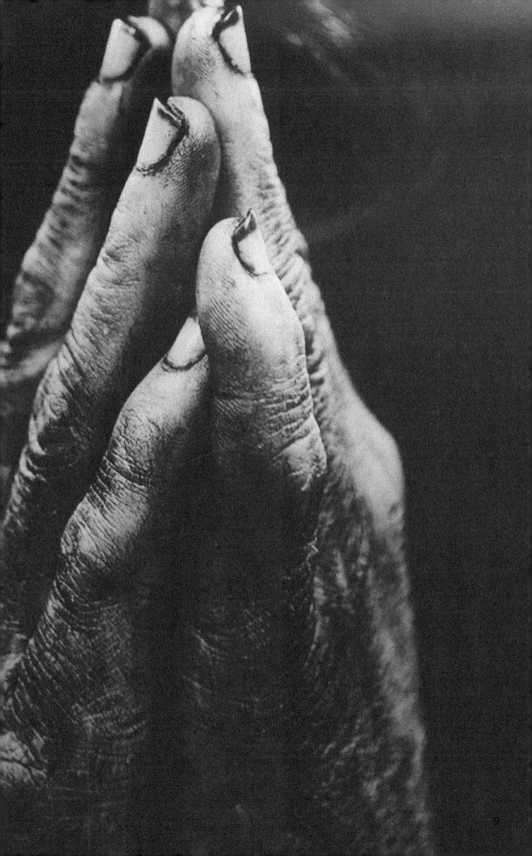

CONFRONTING

YOUR OWN MIND

RELATED READING IN SOUL INVASION: CHAPTERS 1 & 2

WARM-UP: SCRIPTURE AND BRIEF MEDITATION/QUESTION

And you shall love the LORD your God with all your heart, with all your soul, with all your mind, and with all your strength.' This is the first commandment. And the second, like it, is this: 'You shall love your neighbor as your-self.' There is no other commandment greater than these.

MARK 12:30-31

We have Jesus' word the verses above are the bottom line expectation for our lives. The words are so familiar we can say them without thinking – we're on auto-pilot! When asked what they mean, we tend to think, "Well, they mean loving God totally and our neighbors a lot."

What if we were asked to explain the

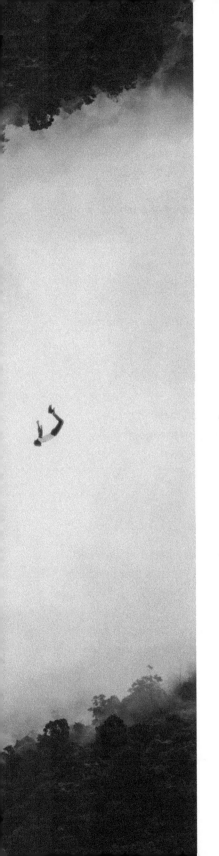

difference between loving God with all our heart and loving God with all our soul? Can we think of examples? Both Matthew and Mark recorded the words above during the last week of Jesus' life, but only Mark included the phrase "with all your mind" in the Great Commandment. This lesson will help you see the mind phrase was clarifying the previous soul phrase. We're not going to get this right until our minds are invaded by God's truth.

Loving God with all your mind is definitely not a no-brainer! Off the top of your head, what are some examples of loving God with all your mind?

READ THE ASSIGNMENT

As you read the book pages for Lesson One (pages 1-25 in *Soul Invasion*), note any questions or observations in the space below. Keep track of marked pages or significant Scriptures you want to remember.

....

....

....

....

....

....

....

....

NOTICE QUESTIONS
WHAT YOU LEARNED AND REMEMBER

- When Pastor Troy wrote, "**Soul Invasion** is not about Easter, but it is about how to live like He's risen when you feel dead yourself" (p.2), what did he mean?

- How does Pastor Troy define the way he is using the biblical word "soul" in **Soul Invasion**? (see page 5)

- What is the difference between thinking the truth sets us free and *knowing* the truth that sets us free? (see John 8:31-32)

- Summarize the thinking and biblical problem that is the theme of chapter 2 "I Am Not Supposed to have Pain."

- Why does God ask questions? (see page 14)

- List the three significant truths Pastor Troy unpacks in these chapters. Which one challenges your thinking the most?

THINK QUESTIONS
WHAT YOU UNDERSTAND AND REALIZE

- On page 7 there were a number of questions listed that were all answered by the principle in Philippians 2:5. What is that principle and how have you seen it work in your life?

- Choose one of the examples of "spiritual jerky" on page 8 and meditate on it for five minutes. Jot down any thoughts the Holy Spirit gave you.

- Can you think of any parallels between the way you currently think and the way the young wife was thinking as Pastor Troy confronted her decision about leaving her marriage? (pages 13-16). How would you describe the lie behind the conclusion that we shouldn't have pain in life?

....

- What did you take away from Pastor Troy's encounter with the witch (pages 19-23) and the way God changes the way we think and see the world?

- Which of the 8 pieces of "spiritual jerky" on page 24 gives you the greatest sense of hope? Why?

APPLY QUESTIONS
HOW YOU WILL APPLY THE TRUTH

- In what areas of your life is God nudging or confronting you about wrong thinking? According to His Word, what do you need to do next?

- Choose one of the verses on pages 9-10. Write in on a card you can post so you can work on memorizing for a new way of thinking. Why did you choose the verse you chose?

- The memory verses on page 25 include John 16:33. If you don't have this one memorized yet, it's time.

- Experiment this week by including your invitation to the Holy Spirit to invade your soul in new ways in your daily prayers.

MOVE TOWARD FREEDOM
A FINAL THOUGHT/CHALLENGE FROM PASTOR TROY

As you begin this study, let Jesus show you how He thinks and you will have certain victory. If you're willing to confront the person between your ears and beat the "in-a-me" into submission, you're at the threshold of walking blessed in a way you never have been before. If you're tired of your thinking realm looking more like a landfill than a place the Lord can spread His goodness, it sounds like you're ready to get some real Biblical answers on how to clean up your mess. You're ready for a *Soul Invasion.*

SESSION 2

FAIRNESS

AND OTHER MENTAL MYTHS

RELATED READING IN SOUL INVASION: CHAPTERS 3 & 4

WARM-UP: SCRIPTURE AND BRIEF MEDITATION/QUESTION

....

But if you have bitter envy and self-seeking in your hearts, do not boast and lie against the truth . . . For where envy and self-seeking exist, confusion and every evil thing are there.

JAMES 3:14, 16 - NKJV

So, what's the problem? It's wrong thinking. It's looking at life based on any set of values apart from God's. And it's taking for granted that our way of thinking must be right instead of realizing our minds are full of myths and misunderstandings our enemy uses to keep us confused.

....

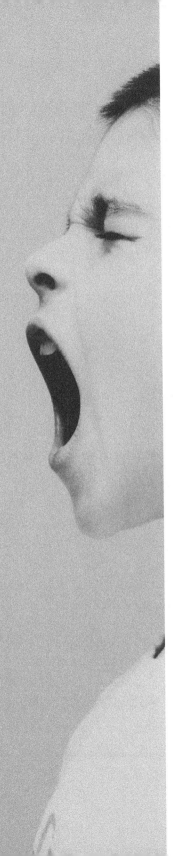

What is your definition of rationalizing and how much do you struggle with this way of looking at life?

READ THE ASSIGNMENT

As you read the book pages for Lesson Two (pages 27-41 in *Soul Invasion*), note any questions or observations in the space below. Keep track of marked pages or significant Scriptures you want to remember.

NOTICE QUESTIONS
WHAT YOU LEARNED AND REMEMBER

- What was the difference between the way Pastor Troy and Leanna looked at the mansions in the neighborhood they visited and the reaction of the band member who didn't even want to drive through there?

- On page 29, Pastor Troy made the statement: "If you want what someone else has, simply do what that person has done to get it." Explain what he meant.

- What is the cure or the "inoculation" for spiritual envy?

- What are the two common myths confronted in these chapters and what truth confronts each one?

- How many specific Scriptures deal with the subject of thinking and why is that important?

- On page 38, how did Pastor Troy use Psalm 8 to teach how thinking about one thing produces something else?

THINK QUESTIONS
WHAT YOU UNDERSTAND AND REALIZE

- How and when do you find yourself tempted to envy others?

- Does knowing what God has for you is always better than what anyone has affect your view of living? What about your view of God?

- What problems do you now see are a result of demanding "fairness" and other myths?

- How does Proverbs 23:7, "For as he thinks in his heart, so is he" remind you of the necessity to control your mind?

- Look up 2 Corinthians 10:4-6 and write out for yourself what those verses mean for believers in Jesus.

APPLY QUESTIONS
HOW YOU WILL APPLY THE TRUTH

- In what ways have you practiced the attitude of wanting what God has for you rather than wishing you had what He has for others?

- How have these chapters helped you recognize and resist the myths that infect your life?

- List at least three positive and three negative ways your understanding of yourself has been shaped by your thinking.

- When it comes to your thought life, in what ways does imagination create problems for you? How can Genesis 6:5-7 help resolve this?

- One of the main points of these chapters is this: "Refusing to conquer our thinking is rebellion against God and it brings judgment." Search your mind/thinking for a few moments. Ask God's Spirit to point out anything in you that expresses this kind of rebellion. If needed, repent.

MOVE TOWARD FREEDOM
A FINAL THOUGHT/CHALLENGE FROM PASTOR TROY

Make up your mind the way your mom used to have you make up your bed. Straighten it out! You are responsible for defending your mind against random thoughts that do not glorify the Lord. You wouldn't let dirty or dangerous things into your home, yet a lot of us let things into our head that we would never allow into any other piece of property we own. You are responsible for defending your thinking against mental intrusions.

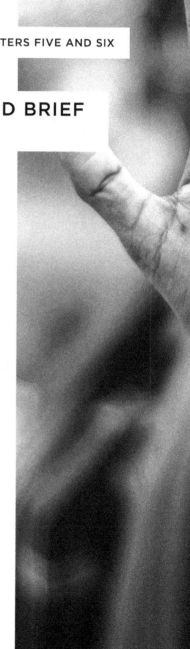

TWO CLASSIC MESSED-UP WAYS OF THINKING

RELATED READING IN SOUL INVASION: CHAPTERS FIVE AND SIX

WARM-UP: SCRIPTURE AND BRIEF MEDITATION/QUESTION

But God proves His love for us in that while we still were sinners Christ died for us.

ROMANS 5:8

There is no greater wedge that Satan can drive between us and our loving Creator than to hint, shout, or insinuate that God doesn't love us. As Pastor Troy puts it, "Every single Christian, everywhere in the world, no matter how loved, has to deal with this thought pattern at different points in their life. If you are smart enough to realize you are greatly loved by God and by whatever

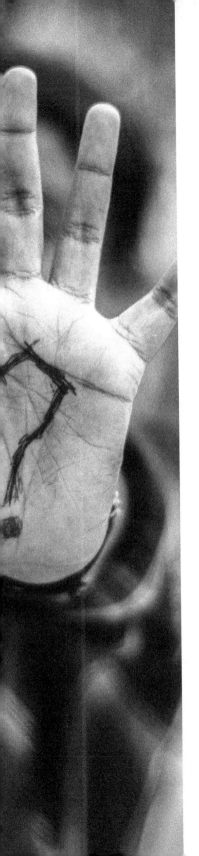

circle of people you are blessed with, the devil will still try to get you to focus on the one or two dummies that should love you and do not." Let's find out how to correct this messed-up way of thinking!

What difference does it make in your life right now that God loves you?

READ THE ASSIGNMENT

As you read the book pages for Lesson Three (pages 43-56 in *Soul Invasion*), note any questions or observations in the space below. Keep track of marked pages or significant Scriptures you want to remember.

....

....

....

....

....

....

....

NOTICE QUESTIONS
WHAT YOU LEARNED AND REMEMBER

- What is the common point made by both 2 Peter 3:9 and Matthew 23:37?

- Pastor Troy wrote: "The rule is not if God wants it to happen it will happen. The rule is that if God wants it to happen and you get with His program, it will happen." What's the main difference between this rule and the earlier messed-up thinking?

- List the three ways the lazy man's vineyard suffered because of his passivity.

- What other parts of life can the vineyard easily represent?

- In chapter 6, what did Pastor Troy mean by the following statement? "When our mental attention is devoted to those that do not love us, our lives become afflicted in every area."

- What does the difference between Leah's first three sons' names and the name Judah tell you about her thinking?

THINK QUESTIONS
WHAT YOU UNDERSTAND AND REALIZE

- When Pastor Troy said, "The vision God has given you can only be achieved by strategic and aggressive action," how did you react to that statement?

- What was wrong with the "half-truth" uttered by Gamaliel (see pages 46-47)?

- In what ways is "leaving it up to God" also a way of blaming God?

- Write out some of the verses that clearly demonstrate that God loves you.

- Why is it significant that the lineage of Jesus that runs through Jacob doesn't run through Rachel, but through Leah, the wife he didn't love?

APPLY QUESTIONS
HOW YOU WILL APPLY THE TRUTH

- In what ways are you currently putting into practice Pastor Troy's statement: "Vision is achieved through strategic action and aggressive moves"?

- Where in your life have been blaming God for something not happening? Do you now see you need to take action and partner with Him to bring about victory?

- Ask God to show you any people in your life who think you don't love them. Seek His help in finding a way for them to experience God's love through you.

- Who are the people in your life you know love you? What do they say about you?

- Take some specific time to praise God for loving you.

MOVE TOWARD FREEDOM
A FINAL THOUGHT/CHALLENGE FROM PASTOR TROY

You can't really love other people until you really understand that God loves you. The greater your revelation of how God loves you, the greater your capacity to demonstrate His love to others. Getting a real revelation of the love God has for you, accompanied by real verbal praise for that love, is the cure to the "nobody loves me" blues.

TWO DANGEROUS

CONCLUSIONS ABOUT LIFE

RELATED READING IN SOUL INVASION: CHAPTERS 7 AND 8

WARM-UP: SCRIPTURE AND BRIEF MEDITATION/QUESTION

....

Be sober, be vigilant; because your adversary the devil walks about like a roaring lion, seeking whom he may devour.

PETER 5:8 (NKJV)

Soul Invasion is not only about changing your mind about certain things; it's really about having God change your mind! We're looking how to change the way we think. We're discovering that if we're not "sober" (serious; not distracted by the things of the world that keep us "drunk" with earthly thinking) and "vigilant" (anticipating attacks rather than hoping they won't happen),

we're going to be in trouble because the devil will eat us for lunch. Fortunately, God wants to change our way of thinking!

READ THE ASSIGNMENT

As you read the book pages for Lesson Four (pages 57-70 in *Soul Invasion*), note any questions or observations in the space below. Keep track of marked pages or significant Scriptures you want to remember.

....

....

....

....

....

....

....

NOTICE QUESTIONS
WHAT YOU LEARNED AND REMEMBER

- What is the key Scripture principle that crushes the idea that "things will never get better"?

- How does the conclusion "things will never get better" reveal distorted thinking about God?

- On page 60, what does Pastor Troy mean by "inventory of hope"?

- How does 1 John 1:3 define two types of fellowship that followers of Christ experience (see page 66)?

- Based on chapter 8, how would you describe a kingdom-minded person?

- On pages 68, what are the three crucial actions that flow out of our participation in the body of Christ?

THINK QUESTIONS
WHAT YOU UNDERSTAND AND REALIZE

- List as many characteristics of the devil and his tactics that you can find on pages 57-58. How does Satan target your mind?

- If you experienced a 1 Peter 3:15 moment today and someone asked you to give reasons for your hope, what would you say?

- How could you use Jeremiah 29:11 to counter your own or someone else's comment that "things will never get better"?

- On page 64, Pastor Troy makes six statements that begin with "A Christian …." Which one of these rings most true in your own life?

- Which one of these statements do you now realize explain some significant issues in your life?

APPLY QUESTIONS
HOW YOU WILL APPLY THE TRUTH

- Which of the Scripture passages on page 62 stirs the most hope in you? Why?

- In what way is your current connection with the body of Christ a healthy expression of spiritual DNA?

- Given that the place for the exercise of spiritual gifts, mutual ministry, and accountability is inside the body of Christ, where do you need to make some adjustments in your involvement with other believers?

- Read the four passages on page 70 several times. What is God saying to you in these comments about the Christian life?

MOVE TOWARD FREEDOM
A FINAL THOUGHT/CHALLENGE FROM PASTOR TROY

A nose is only a growth if it is not in the right place. Perfect as it might be, it still can never be everything it is supposed to be until it is connected to the correct members of the body. Worse yet, the whole body suffers if that nose is rebellious and will not submit to its purpose.

If you are not connected and functioning within the body of Christ, not only are you not all you can be, neither are we. We need you!

STINKIN' THINKIN'

ABOUT GOD

RELATED READING IN SOUL INVASION: CHAPTERS 9 & 10

WARM-UP: SCRIPTURE AND BRIEF MEDITATION/QUESTION

I beseech you therefore, brethren, by the mercies of God, that you present your bodies a living sacrifice, holy, acceptable to God, which is your reasonable service.

ROMANS 12:1

If that verse doesn't make you think twice, you haven't really read it. Some wise guy observed, "The only real problem with a living sacrifice is that it keeps crawling off the altar." This verse isn't about getting the Christian life; it's about living the Christian life. We won't do it apart from the "mercies of God." And God calls our giving Him everything our "reasonable service," just like

it's no big deal — just something simple. Why? Because when we understand that God so loves and so accepts our sacrifice of time, treasure and talent, it does become reasonable. It even begins to make perfect sense!

READ THE ASSIGNMENT

As you read the book pages for Lesson Five (pages 71-89 in *Soul Invasion*), note any questions or observations in the space below. Keep track of marked pages or significant Scriptures you want to remember.

NOTICE QUESTIONS
WHAT YOU LEARNED AND REMEMBER

- How did Pastor Troy explain this statement he made on page 72: "How can God think that it is not that big of a deal for us to give Him all of our life? I'll tell you how. Because He owns it!"

- In what way does 1 Corinthians 6:20 reject the idea that God might ask too much of us?

- What lesson does King Rehoboam's attitude when threatened by King Shishak teach us?

- Why is it folly to think death is after us?

- How did you identify with Pastor Troy's travel story on pages 81-84?

- If death isn't chasing you, who is, and what are you doing about it?

THINK QUESTIONS
WHAT YOU UNDERSTAND AND REALIZE

- What reasons does Pastor Troy give for saying we will be among those singing the song that John wrote about in Revelation 5:9-10?

- On page 74 there is a quote from Rudyard Kipling. What's its point?

- In what ways have you discovered the truth in Pastor Troy's paraphrase of God's statement in 2 Chronicles 12:8, "I'm going to let them serve a tyrant for a while so they can tell the difference between serving me and serving a tyrant" (page 73-74).

- What is your own experience with "heevie-jeevies"?

- On page 85-86, how did Pastor Troy use Revelation 1:17-18 as a key to counter feelings of dread?

APPLY QUESTIONS
HOW YOU WILL APPLY THE TRUTH

- What in your life fits the category of things that would be too much for God to ask for? Why are you holding on to them? Give them to Him and learn to trust.

- How do you know when you are living on the altar of sacrifice?

- Read again over the nine pieces of spiritual jerky on page 77 and choose one to meditate on today.

- In what ways can the verse **"The just shall live by faith"** (Romans 1:17, Gal 2:2; 3:11, & Heb. 10:38) have a greater effect on your life?

- **Jesus said, "Peace I leave with you, My peace I give to you; not as the world gives, do I give to you. Let not your heart be troubled, neither let it be afraid"** (John 14:27). How does His assurance affect your attitude about today or the list above of things you need to entrust Him with?

MOVE TOWARD FREEDOM
A FINAL THOUGHT/CHALLENGE FROM PASTOR TROY

How badly do you want to reach your potential and fulfill your true purpose in life? How intent are you on passing down a blessing instead of a curse? How real is your desire to be clean, victorious and full of the peace of God? Are you hungry for Christ? If so, it will take passionate commitment on your part to keep growing, learning, and moving forward. You will need to be intentional in your thoughts and actions.

You will be required to have a different mentality and an ability to combat your brain when it says, "God wants too much out of me."

It is not too much; it is your reasonable service (Romans 12:1).

MENTAL PRETZELS

ABOUT KIDS AND PLANS

Related reading in *Soul Invasion*: Chapters 11 – 12

WARM-UP: SCRIPTURE AND BRIEF MEDITATION/QUESTION

Not that I speak in regard to need, for I have learned in whatever state I am, to be content: I know how to be abased, and I know how to abound. Everywhere and in all things I have learned both to be full and to be hungry, both to abound and to suffer need. I can do all things through Christ who strengthens me.

PHILIPPIANS 4:11-13

We can certainly get twisted out of shape about our plans, our kids, and our plans for our kids! It's easy to forget the Lord is Lord over all of these things. In theory we know Jesus is Lord; in practice, our frustrations and sadness reveal how easy it is to emphasize the MY in "my plans and my kids" instead of abiding in the truth that my time and my children are both temporary gifts

from God for stewardship, not ownership.

But look at the two times Paul wrote "learned" in these verses. Spiritual gianthood didn't come automatically to Paul—he had to learn these lessons through experience at the school of hard knocks. Just like we do. Fortunately, we have a Lord who is also an amazing and patient teacher.

READ THE ASSIGNMENT

As you read the book pages for Lesson Six (pages 91-104 in *Soul Invasion*), note any questions or observations in the space below. Keep track of marked pages or significant Scriptures you want to remember.

NOTICE QUESTIONS
WHAT YOU LEARNED AND REMEMBER

- What is the picture and lesson from Isaiah 44:1-6 for those who doubt whether their children can be saved?

- What two stages of Jeremiah's life planned by God did Pastor Troy highlight in pages 92-94?

- Why were kings Solomon, Ahijah, and Hezekiah spared by God from total disaster?

- How does the phrase "Blessed are the flexible" harmonize or conflict with your life? Note at least three instances when you have either practiced or failed to practice this truth.

THINK QUESTIONS
WHAT YOU UNDERSTAND AND REALIZE

- Pastor Troy wrote, "I pray that you and I will let the Lord identify us and not let those around us identify us, and certainly not let our pasts identify us" (p. 93). How does this statement affect the way your see yourself and your children?

- What evidence is there that God has marked you and your children for His purposes?

- What conclusions do you draw from these statements by Pastor Troy, "David's faith went past his life. So does yours. David's blessing went past his life, and again, so does yours" (p. 96)?

- Which of the "Pros and Cons" listed on page 100-101 really stood out for you? Why?

- What has been the result of your "It's got to be my way" attitude in your family, your job or your ministry? What is the result of an "I want it to be God's way" attitude?

- Summarize briefly the main lessons you've learned while studying *Soul Invasion* to this point.

APPLY QUESTIONS
HOW YOU WILL APPLY THE TRUTH

- What are you actually doing about any of your children/ grandchildren who might be unsaved? On page 97 are seven pieces of scripture. Turn at least some, if not all, of them into a prayer of trust in God.

- What blessings are you currently enjoying because of the faith of those who went before you?

- There are seven Scripture passages on pages 97-98 that apply to your view of God's plans for your children. Choose one of them to write out and memorize this week.

- In what ways do the lessons from chapter 12 apply to your mindset when it comes to your children? What is your take-home from this chapter?

- Write a note to your children that begins with this thought: "I'm writing you this for when you are a parent yourself. Here are some of the things I have learned about parenting that I now wish I had learned earlier in life. I long to see you please the Lord with your parenting."

- Ask the Holy Spirit to point out for you any areas or plans which you have not declared "Your will be done" in regards to God's right to alter your plans. Wait in silence long enough to let the Holy Spirit speak to you.

MOVE TOWARD FREEDOM
A FINAL THOUGHT/CHALLENGE FROM PASTOR TROY

Your brain has teeth. If you do not command, restrain and control it, it will chew your life to pieces. You can forget about fighting the devil or overcoming the world, until you get real about dealing with what is between your two ears. I call that voice the "in-a-me." It is time for you, as a child of the Most High God, to take back your God-given mental turf with clear Word-based strategies.

GETTING SER

ABOUT A RIGHT MIND

Related reading in *Soul Invasion*: Chapters 13 – 14

WARM-UP: SCRIPTURE AND BR MEDITATION/QUESTION

Then they came to Jesus, and saw the one who had been demon-possessed and had the legion, sitting and clothed and in his right mind. And they were afraid.

MARK 5:15

Jesus was serious about us having a "right mind," as Mark so characterized the restored condition of the demoniac of Gadara once Jesus told his demon tormentors where to go. Jesus was so serious, He didn't hesitate to trade a couple thousand pork chops on the hoof to secure this man's mental freedom. Others were afraid. They had been so afraid of him in his demonized state that

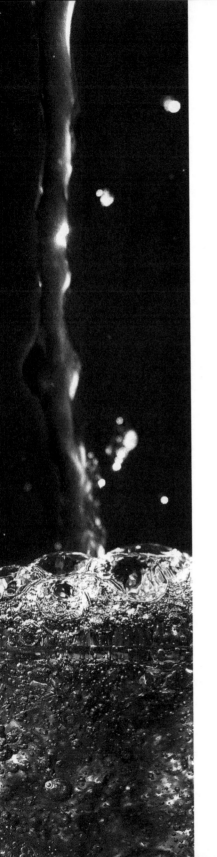

they chained him and confined him in the tombs. Now they were scared because he was normal again – because Jesus had the power to drive out legions of demons with just a word. Jesus comes to set things straight in your life, even if that means that the messed up "order" they were in will get overturned and even destroyed. This is about a soul invasion.

READ THE ASSIGNMENT

As you read the book pages for Lesson Seven (pages 107-123 in *Soul Invasion*), note any questions or observations in the space below. Keep track of marked pages or significant Scriptures you want to remember.

NOTICE QUESTIONS
WHAT YOU LEARNED AND REMEMBER

- What do the words "Armor Up" mean to you especially after reading this chapter?

- Why does every home in Switzerland have a government-issued assault weapon?

- What is the first step required to get your mind ready for battle (p. 110)?

- What is the difference between "truth" and "facts," and why is it important?

- How did Pastor Troy explain the following statement: "there is no neutral in your spiritual gearbox" (p. 120)?

- What did Jesus mean when He talked about "this rock" in Matthew 16 (pp. 120-122)?

THINK QUESTIONS
WHAT YOU UNDERSTAND AND REALIZE

- In what ways have you found Pastor Troy's following statement true: "It is inevitable that you will be spiritually attacked in the area of your mind at some point this very day"?

- Describe two ways you now realize you can increase your level of spiritual readiness for warfare.

- What did you find helpful about Pastor Troy's descriptions of different spiritual "head blows" (pp. 113-114)?

- In what ways might you take encouragement from using the phrase "end of my rope" instead of "ends of the earth"?

APPLY QUESTIONS
HOW YOU WILL APPLY THE TRUTH

- On page 111, Pastor Troy asked three crucial questions: Have you
  allowed the Holy Spirit to personally deal with you concerning your
  mind? Have you let the Lord show you problem areas and potential
  problem areas in your thinking? Do you allow the Holy Spirit to
  convict you in your thinking or is your mind an area you see as off
  limits to God? If you haven't done so already, take some extended
  time to think about and respond to those questions.

- Read through the list of items in the armor issued to you by God
  in Ephesians 6:13-18. Are there any of these you are not actively
  putting on each day? What are you going to do about that?

- Military people describe putting on their armor as "kitting up." Make
  a copy of the nine pieces of spiritual jerky on page 116 and post it
  where you will see it as you prepare for each day.

- Meditate today on the following summary statement from chapter 14:
  "Our ability to find God at our wits' end is based upon our ability to
  seek God at our wits' end."

MOVE TOWARD FREEDOM
A FINAL THOUGHT/CHALLENGE FROM PASTOR TROY

Put your helmet on and fight every battle on the turf that CHRIST JESUS is
within you and you will win every time.

Get your armor on and your defenses up. Don't let the devil have your
mind. It doesn't belong to him. You are protecting the property of the King.

WHAT COMES IN

AND WHAT GOES OUT

Related reading in *Soul Invasion*: Chapters 15 – 16

WARM-UP: SCRIPTURE AND BRIEF MEDITATION/QUESTION

A soft answer turns away wrath, But a harsh word stirs up anger.

PROVERBS 15:1

In chapter 15, we focus on haters and how to respond. In chapter 16, we focus on our mouths and how quickly they can sink our ship. This key proverb brings both themes together, pointing out that our answers to the unprovoked hatred of others must be quiet, steady, and consistent. As we note in chapter 15, the hateful behavior of others is not an excuse for acting poorly ourselves,

and the harsh words aimed at us will be ineffective if we answer them with a wisdom, silence or even kindness.

READ THE ASSIGNMENT

As you read the book pages for Lesson Eight (pages 125-144 in *Soul Invasion*), note any questions or observations in the space below. Keep track of marked pages or significant Scriptures you want to remember.

....

....

....

....

....

....

....

....

NOTICE QUESTIONS
WHAT YOU LEARNED AND REMEMBER

- On page 125, Pastor Troy offers a definition of "haters." What provokes haters to hate?

- When people see the blessings God brings on His people and become envious and even hateful, what are they overlooking (p. 129)?

- What are three significant steps to take in handling haters (p. 130-131)?

- What did you learn in chapter 16 about the meaning of a "two-edged sword"?

- What crucial principle about the mouth does Pastor Troy teach on page 140-141?

- How did Moses use his own mouth as an excuse to avoid God's instructions about going back to Egypt to lead the people out of slavery? (see pg. 141) Did God buy his excuse?

THINK QUESTIONS
WHAT YOU UNDERSTAND AND REALIZE

- When we're hated for any reason, the natural response is to hate back. Why is it crucial to recognize God's view, as Pastor Troy says, "God knows that you have haters and get this; *you are not allowed to become cynical, scornful and distrustful*" (p. 126)?

- When you are tempted to be one of the children of Belial, what can you do for someone that is opposite – or counter-intuitive – of how they act? (see p. 132)

- Why is it important to consider the character and history of critics before we accept the validity of their criticism?

- On page 141, Pastor Troy wrote, "The impulse to speak is always carnal in nature and filthy in substance." What basic human issue is he getting at?

- Describe a time when you discovered the truth of Proverbs 12:6: **"The words of the wicked *are,* "Lie in wait for blood," But the mouth of the upright will deliver them"?**

APPLY QUESTIONS
HOW YOU WILL APPLY THE TRUTH

- One of the spiritual beef jerky statements for chapter 15 was, "If the grass is greener on the other side of the fence, you can rest assured they pay a higher water bill than you." How have you seen this play out in your life or the lives of those around you?

- Review the three aspects of a person who has learned to deal with haters found on page 136. Which of these need to be more present in your life? How?

- As you meditate on Proverbs 18:21 **("Death and life *are* in the power of the tongue, and those who love it will eat its fruit")**, consider if are there relationships in your life which you have brought "death" into through your words. Seeking forgiveness is life-giving. Are you willing to make that powerful move?

- Read the five spiritual beef jerky statements on page 144 out loud. They represent a series of five steps to having your life fully engaged with God. Which step are you on? How can you move forward?

MOVE TOWARD FREEDOM
A FINAL THOUGHT/CHALLENGE FROM PASTOR TROY

When God stands up for His people, it makes other people mad. When you are obviously blessed, it makes other people upset. These are the facts of having life in a world full of death. Know it and learn to deal with it. As I said, "God knows that you have haters and get this; *you are not allowed to become cynical, scornful and distrustful.*"

THE SIZE

AND TEMPERATURE OF THINKING

Related reading in *Soul Invasion*: Chapters 17 – 18

WARM-UP: SCRIPTURE AND BRIEF MEDITATION/QUESTION

He must increase, but I must decrease.

JOHN 3:30

John the Baptist knew something about thinking small. People came to him seeking to provoke envy and competition between him and Jesus. John wasn't having any of that. He knew who he was and who he was not. Another time he said, "Hey, I'm not even worthy to kneel in the dust and tie His sandals." John had a powerful ministry because he knew the power wasn't him;

it was the message and the One who had guided him from the start. Thinking small comes from spending time with and thinking about a big God.

READ THE ASSIGNMENT

As you read the book pages for Lesson Nine (pages 145-166 in *Soul Invasion*), note any questions or observations in the space below. Keep track of marked pages or significant Scriptures you want to remember.

NOTICE QUESTIONS
WHAT YOU LEARNED AND REMEMBER

- Voltaire is a famous name in philosophy. What mistake did he make when it came to God?

- What personal lesson did Pastor Troy learn while seeking the Lord as he camped at Big Bend National Park?

- How many of the nine "little things" from the book of Judges can you remember?

- What kind of thought process does Pastor Troy call a "brain freeze"?

- How would you describe the principle outlined in the following statement: "As already stated, our thoughts control our feelings and many times our feelings control our actions" (p. 158)?

THINK QUESTIONS
WHAT YOU UNDERSTAND AND REALIZE

- How does "getting small" affect the way God works in our lives?

- What is the central point of the 1 Corinthians 1:27-29 quote on pages 153?

- It's one thing to consider all the amazing teaching the Holy Spirit poured out through His servant Paul, but what are some of the lessons we can learn from Paul's character and responses?

- What kind of priceless prosperity does God promise in Joshua 1:8?

- Summarize the main point made by the four Scriptures included on pages 159 (Psalm 19:4; Proverbs 15:26; Jeremiah 4:14; and 1 Chronicles 28:9)?

- What are some of the ways Jesus demonstrated He knows exactly how we think (see pages 163-164)?

APPLY QUESTIONS
HOW YOU WILL APPLY THE TRUTH

-   What experiences in your own life help you understand the benefits
    of being small?

-   Ask the Holy Spirit to point out any places in your thinking you might
    be in danger of wanting to be bigger rather than smaller (Check out
    the spiritual beef jerky for chapter 17).

-   List at least three specific ways you can practice Philippians 2:5, **"Let
    this mind be in you, which was also in Christ Jesus."**

-   How did you answer the following question on page 161: Do you
    have very real mental boundaries set up by the Holy Spirit? How did
    this chapter help set those up or confirm them?

-   Read 2 Corinthians 10:5 again. Take a few minutes to work through
    the process described on page 165: "Pray about it. Ask God to give
    you wisdom in your thinking. Get yourself educated in this area and
    verbally commit your mind to the Lord constantly."

MOVE TOWARD FREEDOM
A FINAL THOUGHT/CHALLENGE FROM PASTOR TROY

Getting still is a matter of prioritizing your relationship with Jesus in such a
way that you are willing to stop and smell the spiritual roses. That means
instead of getting busy with the next thing, you are looking to see where
God's will and word is in the midst of your daily life. God doesn't just say,
"KNOW THAT I AM GOD." He actually says, "BE STILL AND KNOW THAT I
AM GOD" (Psalms 46:10). Prioritize God in the midst of your busy-ness.

CHANGE OF PACE

Related reading in *Soul Invasion*: Chapters 19 – 20

WARM-UP: SCRIPTURE AND BRIEF MEDITATION/QUESTION

I have more understanding than all my teachers, For Your testimonies are my meditation.

PSALM 119:99

In these two chapters, we transition from the practical matters of living with our mind and the way it works to the purposeful matter of settling our mind with God's faithfulness and promises. From God's point of view, there's little difference between a covenant and a promise. The word testimonies in our verse fits both. What God says He will do, He will do. What He says, we can count on. Our best

teachers are the ones who teach us God's ways. We can't rely on God's promises if we never take time to learn or think about them.

READ THE ASSIGNMENT

As you read the book pages for Lesson Ten (pages 167-183 in *Soul Invasion*), note any questions or observations in the space below. Keep track of marked pages or significant Scriptures you want to remember.

NOTICE QUESTIONS
WHAT YOU LEARNED AND REMEMBER

- Which of the six lists was easiest for you to fill out? Which was the hardest?

- Which list ended up being the longest for you? Why?

- At this point in the study, what lesson have you found most helpful? In what way?

- Based on your reading, describe briefly what it means to have a covenant mentality?

- What are the differences between the "ins" and the "ifs" of life (p. 181)?

- On pages 181-182, what three statements does Pastor Troy include that reveal a covenant mentality?

THINK QUESTIONS
WHAT YOU UNDERSTAND AND REALIZE

- Based on Pastor Troy's explanation for using each list you made, which one do you think will be most helpful to you right now?

- What are the main advantages of a covenant mentality?

- Note some specifics from your life that reflect the truth of 1 Corinthians 10:31, **"Therefore, whether you eat or drink, or whatever you do, do all to the glory of God"**?

- How does the lack of covenant mentality explain the lack of commitment and consistency among believers in America today?

APPLY QUESTIONS
HOW YOU WILL APPLY THE TRUTH

- **"A double minded man is unstable in all his ways"** (James 1:8) was noted on page 174 as important information about your mind. Look at the context in James 1:2-8. How can you keep from being double minded?

- Which of God's promises/covenants do you need to keep before you today?

- Read through the "no matter what" statements on 181-182 out loud. How does your life reflect your confidence in God's covenant with you?

- In what ways are you living for the glory of God today?

MOVE TOWARD FREEDOM
A FINAL THOUGHT/CHALLENGE FROM PASTOR TROY

Glorifying God means being occupied with and committed to His ways, rather than your own way. The only way you can do that all the time is when there is nothing in it for you. Your actions are based on covenant, not on need.

KINGDOM THINKING

AND ACTING

Related reading in *Soul Invasion*: Chapters 21 – 22

WARM-UP: SCRIPTURE AND BRIEF MEDITATION/QUESTION

....

But seek first the kingdom of God and His righteousness, and all these things shall be added to you.

MATTHEW 6:33

This is one of the most poorly applied – if not blatantly disobeyed – instructions Jesus ever gave. Not only do we not "seek first;" we often don't seek at all. We ask "when are the 'all these things' going to be added" and forget Jesus made the provision of "all things" dependent on our selling out to the kingdom and His way of living. We realize that when we sell out to God, it will

change the list of "all things" we want added. When God's kingdom and His righteousness are the center of our lives, we actually find the "all things" list gets much shorter and isn't as important. We get closer to the mindset Paul described when he wrote: **"Brethren, I do not count myself to have apprehended; but one thing *I do*, forgetting those things which are behind and reaching forward to those things which are ahead, I press toward the goal for the prize of the upward call of God in Christ Jesus"** (Philippians 3:13-14). Now that's kingdom thinking!

READ THE ASSIGNMENT

As you read the book pages for Lesson Eleven (pages 185-201 in *Soul Invasion*), note any questions or observations in the space below. Keep track of marked pages or significant Scriptures you want to remember.

NOTICE QUESTIONS
WHAT YOU LEARNED AND REMEMBER

- What is the focus of a kingdom mentality?

- How did you respond to Pastor Troy's challenges for Americans in submitting to the truth of the Gospel given our worldview?

- Who gets the credit when you're involved in kingdom things? How important is it for your involvement to be recognized?

- Considering Pastor Troy's thoughts on the more than twenty-year gap between finishing the first 21 chapters of *Soul Invasion* and adding the final three, how would you finish the sentence he was challenged to complete: Jesus is my _____.

- In what ways do you identify with his warnings about Satan's efforts to derail us, particularly the struggle many of us have with anger?

- What are the two kinds of snakes we need to watch out for?

- How do the lessons from Reuben, Samson, and David's life arm us to spot Satan undermining our spiritual sanity?

THINK QUESTIONS
WHAT YOU UNDERSTAND AND REALIZE

- Where have you seen the absence of a kingdom mentality in your own life?

- As you reflect on the lessons found in *Soul Invasion*, what stands out the most for you?

- How did you respond to Pastor Troy's comment about the spiritual warfare armor in Ephesians 6: "When that verse says, 'having done all,' that means you take care of everything you need to take care of so the rest of the battle is all about you standing"?

- What subject did Satan use to get Eve's attention in the garden? How did this undermine what should have been her confidence in God encouraged by Adam?

- How does 2 Corinthians 10:4-5 guide us in preserving supernatural sanity in this world?

APPLY QUESTIONS
HOW YOU WILL APPLY THE TRUTH

- Ask the Holy Spirit to point out any spirit of competition between you and other believers. Give Him enough time to tell you! Ask Him to bless those believers with success; particularly kingdom success!

- Take a moment to meditate on these words from Hebrews: **"Therefore, since we are receiving a kingdom which cannot be shaken, let us have grace, by which we may serve God acceptably with reverence and godly fear. For our God *is* a consuming fire"** (Hebrews 12:28-29). How does this passage affect your response to the uncertainties the world we live in?

- What daily habits (like Leanna's early morning song in her husband's ear) do you find helpful to keep your heart and mind in tune with God? What might be one you could start?

- What are some "snakes" you have talked to in the past that you need to ignore in the future? How will you do this?

MOVE TOWARD FREEDOM
A FINAL THOUGHT/CHALLENGE FROM PASTOR TROY

Reflecting on almost 25 years of God's faithfulness and His lessons, it has seemed appropriate in every way to revise *Soul Invasion* and add some Supernatural Sanity. The spiritual warfare we face is very much in our minds.

You see, weapons are offensive items and the only weapon in the full armor of God is the Sword of the Spirit – the living Word of God. It is mighty for casting down of evil imaginations, arguments, and high things that exalt themselves against the knowledge of God because it is the truth. When you know the truth about the Father, the Son, and the Holy Ghost – when you know how much they love you and have set you up for a great big identity, purpose, and destiny – you can say, "Devil from hell, I'm not listening to you. You are not the author and finisher of my faith. That is Jesus Christ and I'm not going to let My mind go where you want it to. I'm not going to fall for your lies about this situation."

I hope all of this helps you to accept the invitation to have a right mind and one God can work with. May you have dominion in your thinking and peace that passes understanding. It's hard to tell the difference between supernatural peace and supernatural sanity. They are one in the same because they are both Jesus. I impart both to you through these chapters.

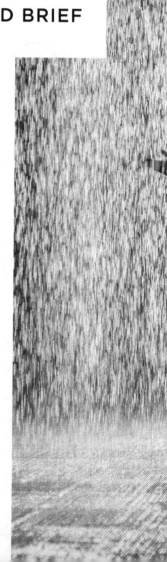

IN WITH THE NEW

OUT WITH THE OLD

Related reading in *Soul Invasion*: Chapters 23 – 24

WARM-UP: SCRIPTURE AND BRIEF MEDITATION/QUESTION

There is no fear in love; but perfect love casts out fear, because fear involves torment. But he who fears has not been made perfect in love.

1 JOHN 4:18

Too often our sins, worries, and fears act as barriers to all God has for us. We should realize God is willing to be the barrier between us and our sins, worries, and fears. He wants to remove them. Instead, we fall for the insane lie that all this stuff must be removed before we can experience God's love and presence. We don't have the supernatural sanity to know that God's

love and presence can drive these things out. It's insanity to keep going through the same motions over and over again while hoping for a different result. Why not let the Lord of the Universe, Jesus Christ, step right into our mess and begin cleaning it up with us rather than trying to do it ourselves?

READ THE ASSIGNMENT

As you read the book pages for Lesson Twelve (pages 203-218) in *Soul Invasion*), note any questions or observations in the space below. Keep track of marked pages or significant Scriptures you want to remember.

NOTICE QUESTIONS
WHAT YOU LEARNED AND REMEMBER

- What is the kryptonite of anxiety? Why?

- How do the brothers Jacob and Esau and their response to God mirror our spirit and soul?

- In Psalm 42:11, what questions does David ask his soul? How does he answer his own questions?

- While the relationship between Jesus' humanity and His divinity is impossible for us to fully understand, what does the Bible make clear about this?

- Think for a minute about everything that happened on the road to Emmaus. Now consider that evening during dinner with Jesus and the two disciples. What moment would you most like to have witnessed? Why? At what point do you think you would have realized it was Jesus?

THINK QUESTIONS
WHAT YOU UNDERSTAND AND REALIZE

- What answer does Pastor Troy provide for the question, "How can you know the difference between your soul and your spirit?" (see page 207)

- How does Pastor Troy explain the difference between *visitation* and *habitation* when it comes to our relationship with God?

- What significant lessons do we need to remember about these two points: 1) Jesus is there when we don't know He is there, and 2) Jesus is with us when we don't know it's Jesus?

- How does the answer to Rebecca's question, "Why am I like thus?" turn out to be the same answer for your question?

- How does the "power of adoration" work, particularly when it comes to depression and the principle of displacement?

APPLY QUESTIONS
HOW YOU WILL APPLY THE TRUTH

- What evidence of supernatural sanity do you know is part of your life today?

- Which of the five statements Pastor Troy keeps handy to speak into his own soul do you think would be most helpful for you to remember? Why? (see page 207-208)

- In the final paragraphs about the struggle between the soul and spirit, what did you find most helpful as you plan to move forward in following Jesus?

- Consider the woman who broke the alabaster box of perfume over Jesus' feet. What do you feel led to do in the next several weeks that would be as radical an expression of unrestrained worship?

- Read the last paragraph of the book one more time. Let the hope and assurance of God's unconditional love for you seep into every corner of your heart and mind.

MOVE TOWARD FREEDOM
A FINAL THOUGHT/CHALLENGE FROM PASTOR TROY

It's an amazing thing when God gives you supernatural sanity. It's a gift and gifts have to be discovered, developed, and demonstrated. Again, if you're full of anxiety, you're not going to discover anything because there's not going to be any creative part of you.

This is not for casual seekers. This is not for people who are just remotely interested in something better and higher. This is for people who want to go deep. There's got to be something going on between you and the Father that's going to change your thinking and set you free, because the Father's desire and His good pleasure, Jesus says, is to "give you the Kingdom." He wants to give you all He owns and He wants to give you dominion. He wants you to have mastery in your life to enjoy and live a life worthy of His blood. He has paid a tremendous price for you to live this life. So live it!

Just remember, sometimes God can be doing an amazing work in your life and you still feel confused. You're still not sure what's going on and you still feel like things are messed up. In those places, you say, "Okay, God. Why am I thus?" And He says, "Because you have a fight on your hands and the war isn't over." The truth is, because of Jesus' death and resurrection, it's ultimately over, but it hasn't all played out yet. We still have to live this life.

SMALL GROUP & LEADER HELP

Resources to make your Small Group experience even better!

FAQS

What do we do on the first night?

Like all fun things in life—have a party! A "get to know you" coffee, dinner, or dessert is a great way to launch a new study. You may want to review the Group Agreement (pages 66) and share the names of a few friends you can invite to join you. But most importantly, have fun before your study time begins.

Where do we find new members for our group?

This can be troubling, especially for new groups that have only a few people or for existing groups that lose a few people along the way. We encourage you to pray with your group, then brainstorm a list of people from work, church, your neighborhood, your children's school, family, the gym, and so forth. Then have each group member invite several of the people on his or her list. Another good strategy is to ask church leaders to make an announcement or allow a bulletin insert.

No matter how you find members, it's vital you stay on the lookout for new people to join your group. All groups tend to go through healthy attrition—the result of moves, schedules, releasing new leaders, ministry opportunities, and so forth—and if the group gets too small, it could be at risk of shutting down. If you and your group stay open, you'll be amazed at the people God sends your way. The next person just might become a friend for life. You never know!

How long will this group meet?

Most groups meet weekly for at least their first eight weeks, but every other week can work as well. We strongly recommend the group meet for the first six months on a weekly basis if at all possible. This allows for continuity, and if people miss a meeting, they aren't out of the loop for a whole month.

At the end of this study, each group member may decide if he or she wants to continue on for another study. Some groups launch relationships for years to come, and others are stepping-stones into another group experience. Either way, enjoy the journey.

Can we do this study on our own?

Absolutely! This may sound crazy, but one of the best ways to do this study is not with a full house, but with a few friends. You may choose to gather with another couple who would enjoy some relational time (perhaps going to the movies or having a quiet dinner), then walking through this study. Jesus will be with you even if there are only two of you (Matthew 18:20).

What if this group is not working for us?
You're not alone! This could be the result of a personality conflict, life stage difference, geographical distance, level of spiritual maturity, or any number of things. Relax. Pray for God's direction, and at the end of this 12-week study, decide whether to continue with this group or find another. You don't typically buy the first car you look at or marry the first person you date, and the same goes with a group. However, don't bail out before the 12 weeks are up—God might have something to teach you. Also, don't run from conflict or prejudge people before you have given them a chance. God is still working in your life, too!

Who is the leader?
Most groups have an official leader. But ideally, the group will mature and members will rotate the leadership of meetings. We have discovered that healthy groups rotate hosts/leaders and homes on a regular basis. This model ensures all members grow, give their unique contribution, and develop their gifts. This study guide and the Holy Spirit can keep things on track even when you rotate leaders. Christ has promised to be in your midst as you gather. Ultimately, God is your leader each step of the way.

How do we handle the childcare needs in our group?
Very carefully. Seriously, this can be a sensitive issue. We suggest you empower the group to openly brainstorm solutions. You may try one option that works for a while, then adjust over time. Our favorite approach is for adults to meet in the living room or dining room and to share the cost of a babysitter (or two) who can watch the kids in a different part of the house. This way, parents don't have to be away from their children all evening when their children are too young to be left at home. A second option is to use one home for the kids and a second home (close by or a phone call away) for the adults. A third idea is to rotate the responsibility of providing a lesson or care for the children either in the same home or in another home nearby. This can be an incredible blessing for kids. The most common solution is to decide you need a night to invest in your spiritual lives individually or as a couple, and to make your own arrangements for childcare. No matter what decision the group makes, the best approach is to dialogue openly about both the problem and the solution.

SMALL GROUP
AGREEMENT

OUR PURPOSE

To provide a predictable environment where participants experience authentic community and spiritual growth.

OUR VALUES

Group Attendance

To give priority to the group meeting. We will call or email if we will be late or absent.

Safe Environment

To help create a safe place where people can be heard and feel loved. (Please, no quick answers, snap judgments, or simple fixes.)

Respect Differences

To be gentle and gracious to fellow group members with different spiritual maturity, personal opinions, temperaments, or "imperfections." We are all works in progress.

Confidentiality

To keep anything that is shared strictly confidential and within the group, and to avoid sharing improper information about those outside the group.

Encouragement for Growth

To be not just takers but givers of life. We want to spiritually multiply our life by serving others with our God-given gifts.

Shared Ownership

To remember that every member is a minister and to ensure that each attender will share a small team role or responsibility over time.

Rotating Hosts/Leaders and Homes

To encourage different people to host the group in their homes and to rotate the responsibility of facilitating each meeting.

OUR EXPECTATIONS

- Refreshments/mealtimes:
- Childcare:
- When we will meet (day of week):
- Where we will meet (place):
- We will begin at (time):_____and end at:_____
- We will do our best to have some or all of us attend a worship service together. Our primary worship service time will be:
- Date of this agreement:
- Date we will review this agreement again:
- Who (other than the leader) will review this agreement at the end of this study:

CALENDAR

Planning and keeping a calendar help ensure the greatest participation at every meeting. At the end of each meeting, review this calendar. Be sure to include a regular rotation of host homes and leaders, and don't forget birthdays, socials, church events, holidays, and mission/ministry projects.

Date	Lesson	Host Home	Dessert/Meal	Leader

PRAYER & PRAISE
REPORT

PRAYER REQUESTS

PRAYER REPORTS

_____ _____

_____ _____

_____ _____

_____ _____

_____ _____

_____ _____

_____ _____

_____ _____

_____ _____

SMALL GROUP
ROSTER

Name	Phone Number	Email	Address	Notes

HOSTING A GROUP
GATHERING

If you're starting a new group, try planning an "open house" before your first formal group meeting. Even if you have only two to four core members, it's a great way to break the ice and to consider prayerfully who else might be open to joining you over the next few weeks. You can also use this kick-off meeting to hand out study guides, spend some time getting to know each other, discuss each person's expectations for the group and briefly pray for each other. A simple meal or good desserts always make a kick-off meeting more fun.

After people introduce themselves and share how they ended up being at the meeting (you can play a game to see who has the wildest story!), have everyone respond to a few icebreaker questions:

- What is your favorite family vacation?
- What is one thing you love about your church/our community?
- What are three things about your life growing up that most people here don't know?

Next, ask everyone to tell what he or she hopes to get out of the study. You might want to review the Small Group Agreement and talk about each person's expectations and priorities.

Finally, set an open chair (maybe two) in the center of your group and explain that it represents someone who would enjoy or benefit from this group but who isn't here yet. Ask people to pray about inviting someone to join the group over the next few weeks. Hand out postcards and have everyone write an invitation or two. Don't worry about ending up with too many people; you can always have one discussion circle in the living room and another in the dining room after you watch the lesson. Each group could then report prayer requests and progress at the end of the session.

You can skip this kick-off meeting if your time is limited, but you'll experience a huge benefit if you take the time to connect with each other in this way.

LEADING FOR THE
FIRST TIME

- Sweaty palms are a healthy sign. The Bible says God is gracious to the humble. Remember who is in control; the time to worry is when you're not worried. Those who are soft in heart (and sweaty palmed) are those whom God is sure to speak through.

- Seek support. Ask your leader, co-leader, or close friend to pray for you and prepare with you before the session. Walking through the study will help you anticipate potentially difficult questions and discussion topics.

- Bring your uniqueness to the study. Lean into who you are and how God wants you to uniquely lead the study.

- Prepare. Prepare. Prepare. Go through the session several times. If you are using the DVD, listen to the teaching segment and Leadership Lifter. Consider writing in a journal or fasting for a day to prepare yourself for what God wants to do. Don't wait until the last minute to prepare.

- Ask for feedback so you can grow. Perhaps in an email or on cards handed out at the study, have everyone write down three things you did well and one thing you could improve on. Don't get defensive. Instead, show an openness to learn and grow.

- Prayerfully consider launching a new group. This doesn't need to happen overnight, but God's heart is for this to take place over time. Not all Christians are called to be leaders or teachers, but we are all called to be "shepherds" of a few someday.

- Share with your group what God is doing in your heart. God is searching for those whose hearts are fully his. Share your trials and victories. We promise that people will relate.

- Prayerfully consider whom you would like to pass the baton to next week. It's only fair. God is ready for the next member of your group to go on the faith journey you just traveled. Make it fun, and expect God to do the rest.

LEADERSHIP
TRAINING 101

Congratulations! You have responded to the call to help shepherd Jesus' flock. There are few other tasks in the family of God that surpass the contribution you will be making. As you prepare to lead, whether it is one session or the entire series, here are a few thoughts to keep in mind. We encourage you to read these and review them with each new discussion leader before he or she leads.

1. Remember that you are not alone. God knows everything about you, and He knew that you would be asked to lead your group. Remember that it is common for all good leaders to feel that they are not ready to lead. Moses, Solomon, Jeremiah and Timothy were all reluctant to lead. God promises, "Never will I leave you; never will I forsake you" (Hebrews 13:5). Whether you are leading for one evening, for several weeks, or for a lifetime, you will be blessed as you serve.

2. Don't try to do it alone. Pray right now for God to help you build a healthy leadership team. If you can enlist a co-leader to help you lead the group, you will find your experience to be much richer. This is your chance to involve as many people as you can in building a healthy group. All you have to do is call and ask people to help. You'll probably be surprised at the response.

3. Just be yourself. If you won't be you, who will? God wants you to use your unique gifts and temperament. Don't try to do things exactly like another leader; do them in a way that fits you! Just admit it when you don't have an answer, and apologize when you make a mistake. Your group will love you for it, and you'll sleep better at night!

4. Prepare for your meeting ahead of time. Review the session and the leader's notes, and write down your responses to each question. Pay special attention to exercises that ask group members to do something other than engage in discussion. These exercises will help your group live what the Bible teaches, not just talk about it. Be sure you understand how an exercise works, and bring any necessary supplies (such as paper and pens) to your meeting. If the exercise employs one of the items in the appendix, be sure to look over that item so you'll know how it works. Finally, review "Outline for Each Session" so you'll remember the purpose of each section in the study.

5. Pray for your group members by name. Before you begin your session, go around the room in your mind and pray for each member by name. You may want to review the prayer list at least once a week. Ask God to use your time together to touch the heart of every person uniquely. Expect God to lead you to whomever He wants you to encourage or challenge in a special way. If you listen, God will surely lead!

6. When you ask a question, be patient. Someone will eventually respond. Sometimes people need a moment or two of silence to think about the question. Keep in mind, if silence doesn't bother you, it won't bother anyone else. After someone responds, affirm the response with a simple "thanks" or "good job." Then ask, "How about somebody else?" or "Would someone who hasn't shared like to add anything?" Be sensitive to new people or reluctant members who aren't ready to say, pray or do anything. If you give them a safe setting, they will blossom over time.

7. Provide transitions between questions. When guiding the discussion, always read aloud the transitional paragraphs and the questions. Ask the group if anyone would like to read the paragraph or Bible passage. Don't call on anyone, but ask for a volunteer, and then be patient until someone begins. Be sure to thank the person who reads aloud.

8. Break up into smaller groups each week or they won't stay. If your group has more than seven people, we strongly encourage you to have the group gather sometimes in discussion circles of three or four people during the Hear God's Story or Change Your Story sections of the study. With a greater opportunity to talk in a small circle, people will connect more with the study, apply more quickly what they're learning and ultimately get more out of it. A small circle also encourages a quiet person to participate and tends to minimize the effects of a more vocal or dominant member. It can also help people feel more loved in your group. When you gather again at the end of the section, you can have one person summarize the highlights from each circle. Small circles are also helpful during prayer time. People who are unaccustomed to praying aloud will feel more comfortable trying it with just two or three others. Also, prayer requests won't take as much time, so circles will have more time to actually pray. When you gather back with the whole group, you can have one person from each circle briefly update everyone on the prayer requests. People are more willing to pray in small circles if they know that the whole group will hear all the prayer requests.

9. Rotate facilitators weekly. At the end of each meeting, ask the group who should lead the following week. Let the group help select your weekly facilitator. You may be perfectly capable of leading each time, but you will help others grow in their faith and gifts if you give them opportunities to lead. You can use the Small Group Calendar to fill in the names of all meeting leaders at once if you prefer.

10. One final challenge (for new or first time leaders):
Before your first opportunity to lead, look up each of the five passages listed below. Read each one as a devotional exercise to help yourself develop a shepherd's heart. Trust us on this one. If you do this, you will be more than ready for your first meeting.

Matthew 9:36
1 Peter 5:2-4
Psalm 23
Ezekiel 34:11-16
1 Thessalonians 2:7-8, 11-12

Want exclusive content?

TroyBrewer.tv

Troy Brewer Ministries offers you the experience of real life and transformation through truth, supernatural teaching and demonstrating the heart of Jesus.

You'll be getting prophetic, spirit-filled teaching.
TroyBrewer.tv is your source for prophetic, spirit-filled teaching 24/7, on any device anywhere in the world. By partnering with TroyBrewer.tv, you can stream hundreds of hours of life-giving, on-demand video, with new programs uploaded each month, including:

- Troy's special conferences
- School of Prophecy and School of Ministry
- Exclusive content, in-depth instruction, special guests and more!

While these teachings will equip you to go after upgrade and find your Kingdom purpose, your TroyBrewer.tv membership is so much more.

You'll be making a difference.
Through the support of your monthly partnership, we free girls trapped in sexual slavery – young women nobody else will help. We redeem them through Answer International, give them the food, shelter, medical help and education they need, then set them on a new path to a life of abundance in Jesus Christ.

Amazing, isn't it? Your partnership will not only build your spiritual defenses, it gives protection and promise to the victims of sexual trafficking in Nepal, India and Belize. So sign up for TroyBrewer.tv today. You'll be transformed and so will they!

ABOUT THE
AUTHOR

When Troy Brewer is not writing books, he is busy recording his worldwide television broadcast "The OpenDoor Experience." His weekly radio broadcast, "Experiencing Real Life with Troy Brewer," can be heard on radio stations throughout the United States and Belize.

On Sundays and Wednesdays, Troy can also be found teaching from the pulpit at OpenDoor Church in Burleson, Texas and leading his tribe of prophetic drop-dead, sold-out Jesus freaks into amazing Kingdom exploits.

He founded the OpenDoor Food Bank in 1995 and still works hard at giving away several million pounds of free food to over 100,000 people every year. He continues to do outreaches to the homeless on a monthly basis – a covenant he's been keeping for 30 years.

When he is not writing, preaching or recording, he is singing love songs to his wife, Leanna, with one of his favorites from his growing collection of guitars.

Leanna is the Founding CEO of SPARK Worldwide, an organization dedicated to Serving, Protecting And Raising Kids throughout the world. Troy serves on the board and teaches pastoral conferences for the pastors in the regions near her orphanages in Africa, Mexico, India, Colombia and other parts almost unknown.

His four kids, Maegan, Benjamin, Luke, and Rhema, all live within a few miles and are building families of their own.

Troy is a descendant of Henry Brewer who fought with Houston for the freedom of Texas in 1836 and is a Texas history junkie.

CONTACT

Email:	tbrewer@troybrewer.com
Snail mail:	301 S. Dobson St., Burleson, TX 76028
Church Website:	OpendoorExperience.com
Ministry Websites:	TroyBrewer.com AnswerInternational.org TroyBrewer.TV
Facebook:	@pstroybrewer
Twitter:	@pstroybrewer
Spark Website:	SparkWorldwide.org

24-hour prayer, resource and sponsorship hotline: **1.877.413.0888**

Troy speaks at a variety of conferences and churches, both domestically and internationally. If you would like to inquire into his availability for ministry, you can contact him through the above information or call the OpenDoor Church offices at 817-295-7671.